THE MESSAGE IS YOU
Guidelines For Preparing Presentations

Association for Educational Communications & Technology

THE MESSAGE IS YOU
Guidelines For Preparing Presentations

Mack R. Rowe

David Curl

Harvey R. Frye

Jerrold Kemp

Wilfred Veenendaal

Association for Educational Communications & Technology
1201 Sixteenth Street, N.W.
Washington, D.C. 20036

Text was prepared by a special committee of the Graphics Interest Group, Association for Educational Communications and Technology.

Mack R. Rowe (chairman) is Chief of Graphic Communications, Federal Reserve Board, Washington, D.C.

David Curl is Audiovisual Consultant, Educational Resources Center, Western Michigan University, Kalamazoo.

Harvey R. Frye is Head, Graphic Arts Department, Audiovisual Center, Indiana University, Bloomington.

Jerrold Kemp is Coordinator, Audiovisual Production Services, San Jose State College, San Jose, Calif.

Wilfred Veenendaal is Assistant Director of Educational Development, Instructional Media Center, Michigan State University, East Lansing.

Layout designed by Mack R. Rowe.

Illustrated by M. David Holman, Art Director, Media Department, Model Secondary School for the Deaf, Washington, D.C.

Editorial Production by G. F. Hipsher.

Contents

Introduction | Foreword

This publication, *The Message Is You,* stems from requests which came from outside AECT. Professional organizations and speakers at conferences asked AECT for the minimal professional standards or guidelines for visualizing presentations. Through its Graphics Committee, the following guidelines were drawn up. The book is designed for simple productions and is intended for people who are unfamiliar with the range of sophisticated materials and devices available for presentations. Dr. Rowe and his committee deserve the thanks of AECT for the work they have devoted to the publication of these guidelines. Such committee work by its members is the real strength of AECT.

— Howard Hitchens
Executive Director
AECT

Many people have responsibilities for presentations at conferences, conventions and other similar meetings. The people involved need guidance in the effective planning and implementation of their presentation duties.

It is the purpose of this material to offer general assistance and to direct you, the reader, to detailed information concerning specific matters relative to the planning, preparation and successful utilization of visualized presentations. In general, we can divide the people responsible into three groups, each with specific tasks which relate to the various phases just mentioned — planning, preparation and presentation.

Accordingly, the material is divided into three major sections. For the PRESENTER (Part I), *Your Ideas are Important,* is written to help you, the person giving the presentation some basic concepts about planning your presentation. You *are* the message. You are a vital part of your presentation. Whether you realize it or not, you are the visual representative of your ideas. As you begin to prepare for your presentation, read this section for your guide to a professional presentation worthy of your ideas.

For the PRODUCER (Part 2), *Producing the Presentation,* is written to assist the person who actually prepares the message in its visualized form. In this case, you are the individual or team of consultants and production specialists who plan and prepare the visual and audio materials which the Presenter will use. This section provides procedures and methods for preparing the basic professional materials for the presentation. Stress is placed on the visual aspect of the presentation since in a large number of cases the Presenter will do the speaking. Accordingly, emphasis is given to the simple presentation. As the Presenter grows in experience, you will most probably demand more sophisticated presentations, e.g., multimage, mixed media, and more information about these can be obtained from the items listed in the bibliography.

For the SPONSOR or HOST (Part 3), *Setting Up For The Presentation,* is directed toward the person or group responsible for making arrangements for the conference itself. You provide the setting for the success of the message. You prepare the framework in which the Presenter can deliver his message. You are the individual or group sponsoring the meeting or offering logistic support for it. This section provides the procedures, scheduling and arrangements for proper support for the Presenter.

In a number of cases, one person may play two or three roles depending on the size of the meeting and the circumstances under which it is given. Therefore, we suggest that you read all three sections. In this way, you will gain a greater understanding of what is involved in putting together a presentation that gets your ideas across.

YOUR IDEAS ARE IMPORTANT

You have spent important time collecting information (ideas) and fitting it together piece by piece into a composite body of information—a system of ideas—your professional content.

You are asked to communicate this assembled and organized information to an audience. You have accepted this invitation because you have a personal or a professional desire to communicate what you consider important information for the audience. You have a communication task which involves the preparation of a presentation.

Costs

Consider what the time and financial investments in your presentation are for you, for the sponsor and for members of your audience. These are outlined below.

Presenter:

$X/hour x no. hours
   planning presentation = $ Cost

$X/hour x no. hours
   for production   = $ Cost

$X/hour x no. hours
   away from home base = $ Cost

              $ Your total
              financial investment

Sponsor:
$ Cost for facilities
$ Cost for equipment required
$ Cost for program staff
$ Cost for publicity

$ Sponsor's total financial
  investment

Audience:

$X/hour x personal   = $ Costs
  productivity time

Travel to meeting   = $ Costs
  costs

$X/hour x presenta- = $ Direct
  tion time x no.   cost
  people

$X/hour x potential = $ Multiple
  no. people   effect
  influenced
  "back home"

            $Audience's
            financial
            and poten-
            tial costs

Realizing these costs, should you not strive to make the best possible presentation?

Effectiveness

You have put much time and effort into selecting and organizing the content of your presentation. Your own accumulation of knowledge and experience with the topic is extensive.

- Shouldn't the quality of your presentation reflect this knowledge and organization?
- Is your ability to make an effective presentation commensurate with your skills in your professional discipline?
- Might you require some professional and technical assistance in preparing an effective presentation?

What follows can help you to consider and to apply many factors that are essential for a successful presentation.

Think about your audience now, not when you finally stand before them. The audience must be considered as much as the content in your presentation.

Information presentation surrounds us each day. Each person in your audience has been exposed to all sorts of presentations. Much of what we see today is the result of a special effort to compete for audience attention. Your audience, therefore, comes to your presentation with certain general expectations about the professional level of your presentation. They expect the quality of the presentation to match the quality of your ideas.

It is not simply a matter of getting before your audience and reading a paper. Words are not enough. Inadequately planned presentations are not enough.

Varieties of Audience

Be alert to the fact that any audience is composed of diverse types of individuals, and it is a challenge to you to reach as many of them as possible. Assuming that the people in your audience came to learn something and are capable of understanding what you will be presenting, there are some problem types you may encounter.

Audience problem-types you may encounter include:

IMPORTANCE OF VISUALS IN A PRESENTATION

Audience Questions

You are asked to serve the audience. Find out about them and what you can do for them relative to your topic. Answers to questions such as these will provide clues for your topic:

1. What level of interest does the audience probably have about your topic?
2. Is your purpose to motivate or to inform?
3. Is the group naive or sophisticated in its knowledge of the topic?
4. Is the audience better prepared for an overview or for a report in depth?
5. What does the sponsor expect you to do with the audience?

When you determine answers to these questions you will know a great deal about the characteristics and expectations of the audience and how you should approach your topic to best serve them.

Notice that we are using the term "presentation" rather than "speech" or "talk". A presentation denotes more than just words, and it is an unusual person who can be interesting and truly effective without some visual support. The very nature of our language, with the limited experiences of most people, often makes it difficult to convey ideas and information efficiently without resources beyond words.

Visual materials, even words projected on the screen, have a particular strength in communication. They compel attention. Carefully selected and prepared still and motion pictures can overcome the limitations of time and space, helping the audience to understand things which are too big, too small, too far away, too ancient, too slow, too fast, or too complex, for nonvisual comprehension. Visual support can help sustain thought continuity and organization of ideas in a presentation.

There is much evidence that people not only understand but retain what they see and hear significantly longer than that which they only hear.

Include Visual Ideas Early

If you agree that visual support is necessary in your presentation, don't wait until you have the verbal message planned to then begin considering pictures which can "pretty up" the story. In your planning, decide where visuals can carry ideas and supply understandings. Then integrate the visual and verbal ideas as you develop your presentation.

You may save time by using visuals which permit expansion and restatement of your more important concepts.

Planning is necessary to give a professional presentation. Planning and producing a presentation usually take more time than expected. Give yourself plenty of advance time. Start planning early, particularly if the process is new to you.

Editing is Advisable

An audience can absorb only so much in a given time period. Try putting yourself in their place. It more than likely will not be possible for you to use all your content within your time allocation. Be selective with content so that only the most important and useful information, in terms of audience needs, is included.

More detailed or technical ideas can be reserved for handout materials such as reprints or copies. These handouts can be complete texts or bibliographies. If much material is to be covered, it would be well to consider an intermission or a second meeting.

Ask yourself, "What do I want to accomplish with this audience?" If your answer is "to inform," that is not enough. It is better to ask yourself, as well as the sponsor, "What do I want my audience to learn or to want to do when I am finished with my presentation?" Write your objectives down: "Change attitude about," "Change behavior toward," "Direct to," "Give basis for decisions." Then ask, "Can I reasonably expect to do this in the time I have?"

These questions will help you realistically plan what parts of your content can be included and what parts must be deleted or handled in other ways.

Organize the Selected Information

After you have selected the major points for your presentation, organize them sequentially. This becomes the content outline. The consideration you have given to audience factors and your objectives will cause you to organize ideas differently from your usual way.

Do not spend a great deal of time refining the development of the presentation at this phase. The next phase involves the integration of visual or pictorial information and may cause further changes in the sequence of ideas.

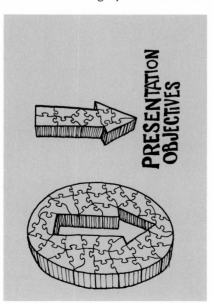

THE STORYBOARD — A TOOL FOR PLANNING

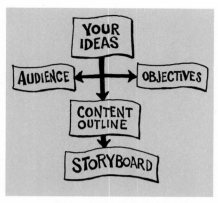

A storyboard is a convenient and very helpful part of the planning process. It is a way to help you think about the development both of the visuals and the text in relation to each other. A more effective presentation can be created by thinking of visuals at this point, rather than by writing a speech and then trying to visualize it paragraph by paragraph.

"Tacked-on" visuals will usually lead to a slow-moving presentation which often appears to be poorly organized.

The storyboard will also serve well as a means of communication with anyone working with you designing or producing the presentation materials.

Using the Storyboard

A very flexible storyboard can be made by placing each separate

idea on an individual index or file card (4" x 6"). Each card can be planned so that it has specific areas designated for text ideas and for pictorial ideas, which can be roughly sketched. The cards can be organized into different idea sequences.

During this organization process you can quite easily rearrange the transitions and relationships between ideas so that a continuity for your presentation will emerge.

It would be to your advantage to now work with a producer (described under "Visualizing Your Ideas") planning with the storyboard. Cooperation at this time would be to his advantage, too, if you will be needing his production help.

MEDIA FOR YOUR MESSAGE

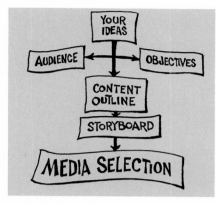

The next step is to select a medium for presenting your ideas. Most of the media mentioned below are best suited for pictorial presentation. However, limited amounts of verbal information can also be presented with them. The following characteristics can help you determine which medium is best for you:

1. The overhead projector (uses transparencies)
   - Used in front of room with you; allows you to face your audience.
   - Room can be semi-lighted.
   - You can control the development of ideas directly.
   - Ideas can be progressively presented with exact timing by using overlays. New ideas can be introduced without changing the overall image.
   - Notations can be added during the presentation.

2. The 2 x 2 (35mm slides) projector
   - Can be easily controlled by you or an operator.
   - Good for showing photographic pictures.
   - Can be synchronized with sound tape.

3. The motion picture projector
   - Particularly good when motion is inherent to an idea.
   - Parts or "clips" can be shown.

4. Audiotape recorder
   - Can add interviews or special sounds to the presentation.

5. The flip chart
   - Good with small groups.
   - Preparation of the large pages is often laborious; as is transporting them.

6. Closed-circuit TV
   - Good when presenting to several groups in different locations.
7. More than one medium
   - It may be to your advantage to consider more than one medium for your presentation.
   - Two projectors simultaneously for comparisons or orientation.
   - Interjection of another (such as motion picture clip) for special explanation.

How large an audience do you anticipate? The size of the group and the kind of room often determine the kinds of visual media you will use. With a small group, an informal presentation with simple flip charts may be suitable. But projected materials in a more formal setting are required with a larger audience.

Can the room be adequately darkened? There is no use planning to use slides if the room cannot be darkened so that the audience can see the visuals satisfactorily.

VISUALIZING YOUR IDEAS

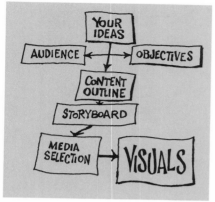

There are many art, photographic, drafting and AV materials available for making visuals. With many of these it is possible for you to do the preparation work yourself.

On the other hand, you may want to have someone else help you produce your visuals. A producer in this case is a communication specialist such as may be found in an audiovisual department, a graphic design department, or a commercial art department. He can be helpful in making suggestions for designing your visuals. Try to consult such a person while you are in your planning phases.

Types of Visuals

There are a number of different types of pictures from which you may want to make selections for your presentation. Your communication specialist may be able to produce them or have them produced for you. The following outline of categories, while not complete in its ability to neatly classify all pictures, may serve as a useful guide for thinking and discussion.

In general, pictures may be classified as photographs, illustrations and words (or numbers). A picture can be created to perform different communication functions.

	Photograph	Illustration	Words and Numbers
Expository	General scenes. Medium and long shot views. Usually single image, in focus, straight-forward observation.	Same as photo, but done with line drawing, washes, painting, woodcut, engraving.	Titles, content outline components, brief general statements.
Interpretive	Special emphasis given via soft or selective focus, lens distortion, lighting, use of subjective camera, image super-imposition, selection of subject angle and pose.	Same as photo, but done with techniques outlined above.	Special words used for emphasis, also special type faces. Poetry.
Technical	Specialized views; closeups; step-by-step sequences; cutaways; exploded views; photos in charts, maps, diagrams; models.	Same as photo plus anthropometric and technical drawings, blueprints, schematics.	Word diagrams and schematics, new concept introduction, formula, table.

Expository: Visual description of people, places, events, and things with emphasis on a general kind of statement of these.

Interpretive: Visual description of people, places, events, and things with emphasis on conveying feelings, emotions, evaluation, symbolism, and/or particular characteristics.

Technical: Visual description of people, places, events, and things with emphasis on specialized, detailed information statements.

PRODUCTION REQUIREMENTS

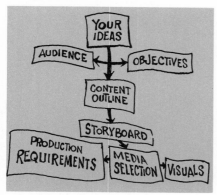

PRODUCING THE PRESENTATION

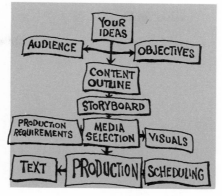

Production Services

There are various services available for the production and reproduction of presentation materials. All of them may not be available in a given locality. All will probably not be useful in solving your particular presentation problem. A communication specialist will be helpful in locating and utilizing people who provide these services:

1. Illustration art: Individuals have various titles depending on the type of art they produce: painter, illustrator, cartographer, draftsman, photographer, calligrapher (lettering specialist), technical illustrator.

2. Photography: Various types of interpretive, expository and technical photographs can be taken depending on the person and the equipment available.

3. Audio: A sound specialist is a technician in a studio or with privately-owned equipment providing recording and playback services.

4. Printing, duplicating, transparency making: Printing and duplicating shops, as well as some offices, can provide services.

Printed copies: spirit duplication, mimeograph, offset, lithography, electrostatic, thermographic.

Transparencies: electrostatic, thermographic, diazo, photographic.

A storyboard will provide a good means of communication with the producer.

Plenty of time should be allowed so the specialist or artist has time to do his work. Let him read this article so all persons working on the presentation have the same orientation to your presentation. Explain the purpose of your presentation and of each visual to help him make good decisions for the production process. Tell him the who, what, when, and where of your presentation, the kind of audience and the size. Give the producer some freedom to make suggestions to improve your storyboard sequence or the kinds of pictures you might use.

Make final selection of the medium or media which you can use or learn to use comfortably and for which the producer can best make materials. He may be equipped for only certain kinds of production. Determine whether or not you will need handouts and how they shall be duplicated.

Set up a schedule with the producer that he can realistically meet. Allow yourself time to review the visual materials before final production. Changing or correcting the art takes time. Also, allow time to rehearse with the materials before you leave for the convention.

It is well at this point to make sure you and the sponsor have made contact, have scheduled for your presentation, and have arranged for whatever meeting and presentation facilities you will need.

Throughout and at the end of the production process, ask yourself the following questions in order to evaluate the visuals:

1. Do the visuals effectively help me reach my goal(s) with this audience?

2. Will each visual effectively help me make my point? Will I need to rewrite parts of my script so it relates to the visual?

3. Is the information in each visual clear and accurate?

4. Do the visuals relate to each other in a consistent way (e.g., terminology, color coding, letter styles)?

5. Do the visuals develop systematically?

6. If necessary, do I have time to make changes in a visual?

GETTING READY

WHEN YOU GET THERE

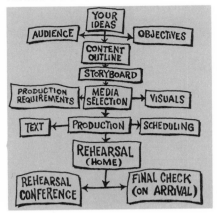

The final stage of preparation for your presentation is a rehearsal to make sure everything works together.

Be sure all your materials are ready and in order — slides, overhead transparencies, tapes, film clips, charts. Is enough equipment available for a dry run? If not, improvise. For example, you can place transparencies on a lightbox by hand if an overhead projector isn't handy.

Run through the entire presentation several times. Ask colleagues to make suggestions. Tape-record each dry run and critique yourself. If you can do this on videotape, you'll get an even better idea of how it will appear to the audience.

Check the timing. Be sure each visual comes when it should for maximum effect and leaves the screen when you proceed to the next point. Do not exceed the time allotted for your part of the program.

Be sure visuals and text work together — not redundant, not verbose. Sometimes it is worthwhile to reinforce portions of a visual by reading. But do not insult the intelligence of your audience by repeatedly reading to them what they can read for themselves.

Be sure all visuals are clear and legible from as far from the screen as the last row of viewers is likely to be.

Determine whether you need to give special instructions to a projectionist on sequence or timing of the visuals.

When you arrive at your meeting or conference, several steps are important to insure a smooth performance.

1. Find out when the schedule will allow you to get set up. Be at least an hour early, or before the previous meeting, if possible.

2. Familiarize yourself and your supporting crew with the facilities and equipment. Inspect everything that is to be used:

General:
☐ Right subject and title?
☐ Sequence in program checked?
☐ Inspected for cleanliness and condition?

Slides:
☐ Mounts compatible and straight?
☐ No dirt or fingerprints?
☐ Orientation checked so that each slide goes on the screen properly?
☐ Magazines tested for jamming?
☐ Prefocused and framed?

Transparencies:
☐ Proper sequence?
☐ No dirt or fingerprints?
☐ Proper orientation for screen?
☐ Projected image contained on screen and not spilling over?
☐ Overlays operating properly?
☐ Focus okay?
☐ No screen blockage by projector or by you?
☐ Projected image straight on screen?

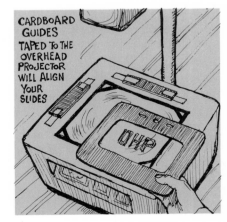

CARDBOARD GUIDES TAPED TO THE OVERHEAD PROJECTOR WILL ALIGN YOUR SLIDES

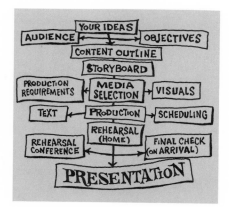

Films:

☐ Heads out, wound properly?
☐ No breaks, tears or weak splices?
☐ Sound: optical, magnetic or silent?
☐ Run down to titles?
☐ Prefocused and framed?
☐ Sound level determined?

Tapes:

☐ Heads out, wound properly?
☐ Speeds checked?
☐ Tracks compatible?
☐ Playback level determined?
☐ Cued up?

3. Run through the entire presentation if time allows; otherwise, rehearse the opening and closing and key transitions between different media. Ask someone to sit in the audience position to react to visibility, lighting and sound level. Be sure change cues are understood by the projectionist, audio technician and others.

The presentation should go smoothly if it has been well organized and rehearsed. But be ready if something does go wrong. Above all, don't get flustered and don't apologize. Continue as if nothing happened. Make on-the-spot changes and ad lib if you have to. Unless you falter, the audience may never realize that anything has gone wrong.

Afterward

Sit down after your presentation to critique yourself honestly. Don't depend entirely for feedback upon the handshakes and back-slaps of friends and colleagues, but listen instead to a taped replay of your presentation. Ask pointed, specific questions later, if you can, of people who were in the audience. Could they hear everything that was said? Could they read the visuals? What about the pacing? How would they have done it?

Confidence comes from experience. Everyone has butterflies in his stomach when facing a large group, even professional performers. Getting through an important presentation successfully should help give the strength, skill and determination to try again.

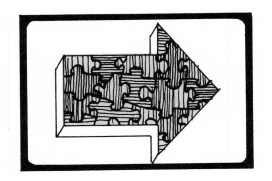

PRODUCING THE PRESENTATION

This part deals specifically with the design and production of visual materials for presentation. The intention is to provide guidelines for a particular presentation. More detailed publications for further information are listed in the bibliography. We can begin by dividing production for the presentation into two basic areas: visual materials and handout materials.

VISUAL MATERIALS DESIGN

A basic design principle for a visual is simplification. A visual does not have to be completely detailed to stand alone. You will be there to explain it.

Limit each visual to a single idea. The confusion potential introduced by too many ideas tends to reduce its impact and retention.

Plan the amount of information you want the audience to see in a visual at any given time in your presentation. If you show more than is necessary, they will tend to be farther along in the presentation than you are ready for them to be. With slides (and flip chart sheets) the information can be split into a sequence of several slides (or panels). With overhead transparencies, the information can be split into a series of overlays.

Pictures

In planning visuals, convert your information to pictorial form whenever possible, e.g., tables into charts, text into brief outlines. Try to keep the picture styles consistent throughout the presentation. Include only those details which are relevant to your presentation message, e.g., minimum number of curves, lines, and bars. More detailed information is best handled as a handout distributed for later study.

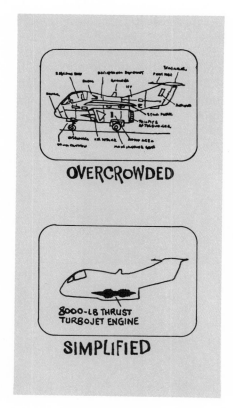

OVERCROWDED

SIMPLIFIED

Charts, maps, diagrams, and technical drawings can be presented in either negative or positive form. Color can be used for emphasis and/or coding as can shading. Symbols should be used in strong contrast to the background and should be large enough to be easily read.

Photographs, cartoons and illustrations can best be presented in positive form, unless special effects are desired. Color and shading can be used for emphasis, coding or realistic description. Be sure not to distract from the main point of the picture by using too much color. Use closeups in photos to show specific details clearly.

Varying line thicknesses in drawings can focus attention and indicate importance. Some items are more important than others and need to be emphasized with thicker lines. A picture may be more visually interesting as well as more easily read when it is enhanced by a variety of line sizes.

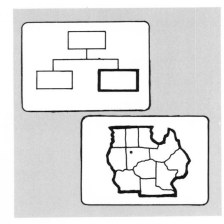

Words

Verbal information, when properly handled, can become a very useful visual. Use key words, not complete sentences. Outlines should consist of no more than five or six items, one item per line. Spacing between lines of type should be 1 to 1½ lines.

Organize letters in straight lines only. Do not stairstep or stack letters, as it impairs readability. Group the words so that they are visually related in appropriate idea groupings. This prevents improper association in the reader's mind.

All lettering should be large enough to be read by people seated at the back of the room or on the extreme sides. Typewriter type is often too small for projection, as are captions printed in books. Primary typewriter lettering will be large enough but rather ragged looking.

Mechanical lettering aids are helpful for a professional look but take more time.

Hand lettering is fast and works well if it is stylized and in straight lines to give it an overall consistency. One-quarter inch height is readable type in most situations. A grid is provided in the Appendix and is useful as a hand-lettering guide.

Use letter styles which are easily readable. The sans serif types are most useful. When special effects are desired, other styles may be used sparingly.

NEGATIVE

POSITIVE

PHOTO

CLOSEUP PHOTO

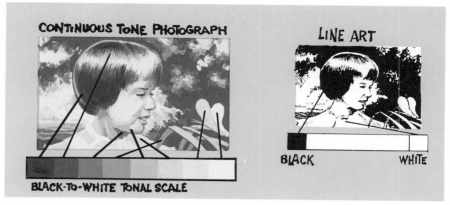

CONTINUOUS TONE PHOTOGRAPH

LINE ART

BLACK-TO-WHITE TONAL SCALE

BLACK   WHITE

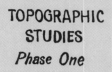

TOPOGRAPHIC STUDIES Phase One

KARST TOPOGRAPHY

ONE LINE

TYPEWRITER
ABCDEFGHIJKLMNOPQRSTUVWXYZ
abcdefghijklmnopqrstuvwxyz
1234567890

PRIMER TYPEWRITER
Primer Typewriter

• IBM Directory Type
qwertyuiop‡ QWERTYUIOP&
asdfghjkl'= ASDFGHJKL'+
zxcvbnm,.- ZXCVBNM:;
$1234567890% #*¶/$†?!¢()@

'MECHANICAL'
ABCDEFGHIJKLMN
OPQRSTUVWXYZ&
1234567890

HANDLETTERING
ABCDEFGHIJKLMN
OPQRSTUVWXYZ

 E SERIF   E SANS SERIF

GEOSYNCLINE   FAULT

Kinds of Art

For production purposes the original art can be divided into continuous tone and line categories. Understanding these continuous tone and line categories helps determine the method used for converting (reproducing) art into a projectable visual.

Continuous tone art includes illustrations, paintings, photographs, and magazine pictures which have shades of grey or variations of color in the image. Color is included because there are different values in colors which would convert to different greys in black and white photographs.

Line art includes charts, maps, diagrams, music which have no greys. The image is made up of black lines on a white background or vice versa.

Art Materials

The material on which the original artwork is sketched, drawn or produced is opaque, translucent or transparent. A table is provided in the Appendix on the copying processes which can be used with these different materials to produce projectable visuals.

Opaque artwork is produced on materials which reflect light rays. It is necessary to convert this art to transparent form for projection. Opaque materials are such things as photographic paper, cardboard and tearsheets. The largest amount of original artwork falls in this category. Conventional art pens, inks, pencils, and photos are used to produce the original images on these materials.

OPAQUE

TRANSLUCENT

TRANSPARENT

Translucent artwork is produced on materials which are partially transparent — they transmit some light and reflect some light. It is also necessary to convert this art to transparent form for projection. Examples of translucent materials are tracing paper and frosted acetate. Conventional art pens, inks, pencils, and photos are used to produce the original images on these materials.

Transparent artwork is produced on materials which permit light to pass completely through them. This kind of art can often be used directly in projection. No copying process is necessary. Clear acetate is the best material to use. Appropriate color sheets, tapes, pencils, markers, and inks which are transparent and which stick to the acetate must be used.

Lines can be scratched on a transparent surface with a compass point and will project as fine, dark lines. This technique is good for chart and table grids. Opaque paper shapes or real objects will project as silhouettes when adhered to clear acetate.

SCRIBING ACETATE

The Readable Visual

The original art, which can be copied to produce a slide or overhead projector transparency, may be created in a variety of ways. Most generally, the art work will be in opaque form to be transformed into a slide. One of your primary concerns will be to prepare the art so that all details will reproduce well and will be readable in the projected visual.

The readability of an illustration to be reproduced for black and white projection can be assured if executed in a reproducible grey scale. The artist can plan for detail clarity before the photographer converts the original to slide form. This is very important

ORIGINAL ART

COPYING PROCESS

PROJECTABLE VISUAL

when preparing materials for television. When working with color, the medium used and the hue, value and chroma of each color used in the original artwork will greatly affect the resulting color slide or transparency. The strengths and weaknesses of color film in reproducing the desired colors for slide projection must be understood. Photographic tests of color used followed by the application of predictable standards will lead to greater control in developing final artwork which will read well in the projected visual. Learning to "paint for the film" in preparing a color illustration is extremely important.

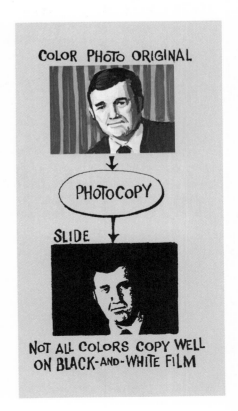

COLOR PHOTO ORIGINAL

PHOTOCOPY

SLIDE

NOT ALL COLORS COPY WELL ON BLACK-AND-WHITE FILM

Readability of a continuous tone black and white or color photograph is determined by the photographer's approach to the subject matter. The message of the photograph is effectively controlled through careful manipulation of camera angles, cropping and lighting.

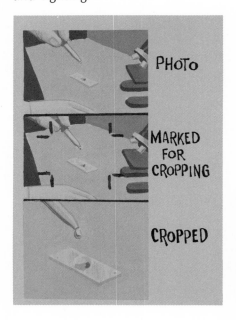

PHOTO

MARKED FOR CROPPING

CROPPED

It is always important to keep in mind figure-ground relationships. What should be emphasized? What should be subdued? Keep message-carrying elements dominant and subdue those of secondary importance.

Even the best photograph can be improved by retouching. Careful retouching draws the eye to the important elements of a visual, clarifying detail using contrast to develop separation, strengthening lines, subduing orientation or supplementary materials, or removing distracting elements. Insets showing magnification, added arrows and other emphasis-giving techniques may clarify picture content.

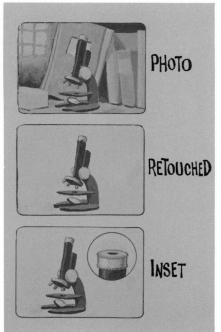

PHOTO

RETOUCHED

INSET

The readability of original line art in black and white or color is relatively easy to control during production and copying processes. Color can be added by dyes, markers or color sheets after an overhead transparency is made or before a color slide is shot.

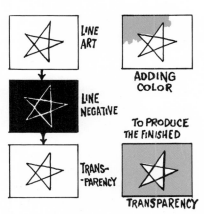

LINE ART

ADDING COLOR

LINE NEGATIVE

TO PRODUCE THE FINISHED

TRANS-PARENCY

TRANSPARENCY

Art which combines continuous tone and line materials is usually copied on a slide. To insure readability of this art on a projected slide, it may be necessary to use a combination of techniques in creating the visual. There are many ways to combine a black and white photograph with drawn diagrams, to use an illustration as a background for a title slide, to use a drawing over a colored photograph, etc.

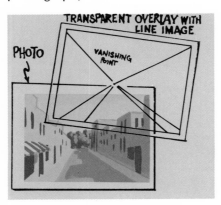

Standardized Art

Art production is quite often facilitated when you use a standardized format size. Not only are the copying, handling and filing problems reduced, but also the finished visuals are consistent in readability and quality.

The primary material for artwork is the base. It should be larger than the art to allow room for registration marks, notes, handling, and sequence numbers. The base is cut from a piece of 10" x 12" cardboard or paper which will serve as base for all art images and overlays.

The base serves to hold the next layer — the art. The art can be an 8" x 10" photo or an 8½" x 11" illustration, painting, or drawing.

A projection frame line is an imaginary line which defines the image area on the art which is to be copied on a slide or a transparency. The projection frame line is smaller than the overall art size, so that the image still fills the slide frame in the event the projection frame area is not copied exactly. The projection frame should be in proportion to the projection frame dictated by the particular projector you will use:

- Single frame filmstrip, motion picture frame, TV frame: 6.47" x 8.5"
- 35mm slide frame: 5.75" x 8.5"
- Overhead projection frame: 7.5" x 9.5"
- Lantern slide projection frame: 2.75" x 3"

Allow a reading space line between the projection frame line and any wording or other important visual information. Projection frames vary somewhat with different brands of projectors. Thus, the reading line is an insurance that all important information will be seen on the screen and inside the frame. It is irritating to try to read information which touches or goes outside the frame. Set the reading space line one-half to three-quarters of an inch from the frame line.

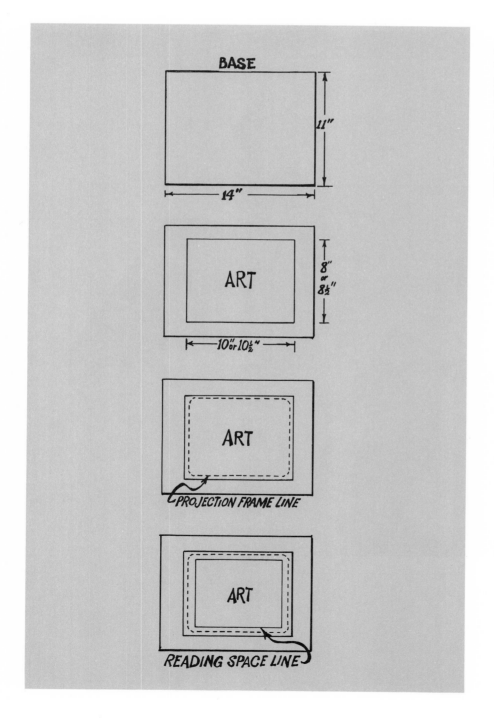

Schedule with the printer or duplicator while the handout art-work and typing are in production so he can schedule to print in time. The communication specialist can also supervise the production of this kind of art. A summarization table briefly outlining some pertinent information for getting your handouts produced is given in the Appendix.

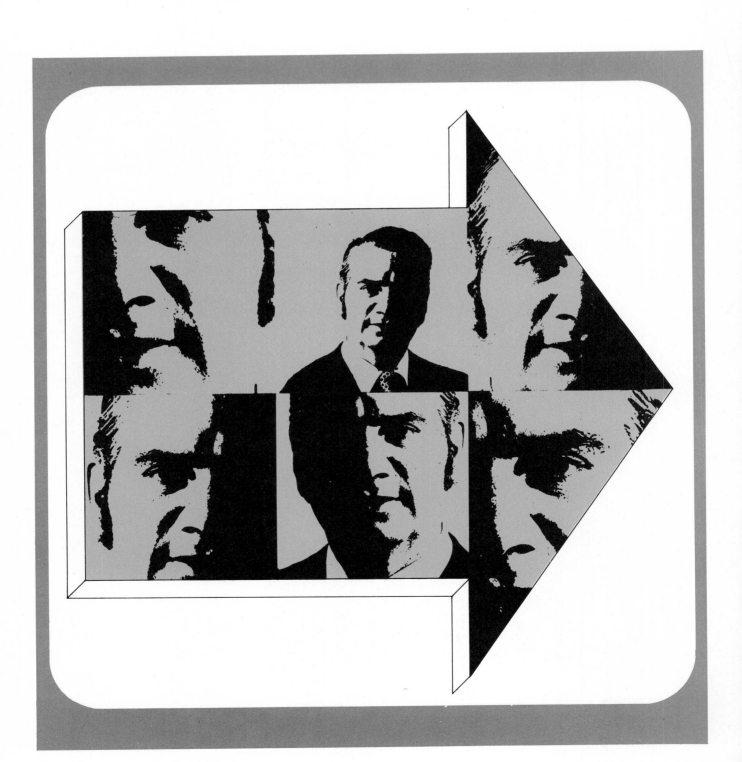

SETTING UP FOR THE PRESENTATION

This section discusses in detail the recommended considerations for the service and support functions of the sponsor before, during and after the conference.

At the outset you might consider it worthwhile to send each person on your agenda who will be giving a presentation at least one copy of this article as soon as possible. Each may want a second copy to give to his producer.

As you plan your presentation facilities, ask the following questions as they become appropriate.

MEETING ROOMS

Size
- Is the room large enough for the anticipated audience?

Seating
- Will there be enough chairs, tables, etc.?
- Are the exits free? Exit lights okay?

Screen Viewing
- Can the audience be arranged for best viewing of the screen? (Consider pillars, doorways, and aisles.)
- Is the front row of seats no closer than two screen widths?
- Is the last row no farther than 6 screen widths?
- Is no row of seats wider than its distance from the screen (except wide-screen)?

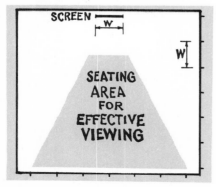

- Is the image bright enough for people in the side seats?
- Is the image distorted?
- Will everyone be able to see when the seats are filled?
- Is the ceiling high enough for placement of a screen of the proper size?
- Do you need horizontal, vertical or square format?
- Is keystoning eliminated?
- Is the surface appropriate for viewing conditions?
- Are chandeliers, decorations and pillars interfering?
- Have stage curtain controls been tested?

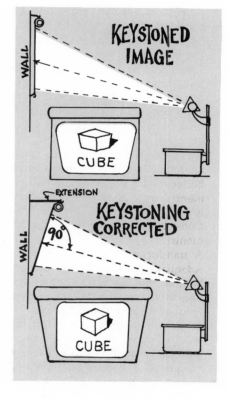

- Should rear-screen projection be considered?

Consider the following advantages: The projector is out of view of the audience. No one can stand in front of the projection beam and cast a shadow on the screen. There is no need to create a center aisle for a projector. More seating at the optimum center of the screen axis is possible. The room can be semi-lighted. Thus, the screen image better relates to the room environment than it does when the room is completely dark.

Consider the following requirements:

A translucent screen is necessary. Adequate space must be allowed behind the screen to allow the projected image to fill the screen. Front-surfaced mirrors can fold the projection beam and shorten the required space, as can wide-angle lenses. The area behind the screen should be as dark as possible.

- If screens are not available, can large white paper sheets be taped to the walls?

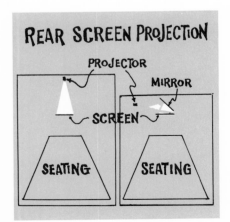

REAR SCREEN PROJECTION

PROJECTOR

MIRROR

SCREEN

SEATING   SEATING

Comfort Control
- Will heating, air conditioning or ventilation systems be adequate for the size of the group? (Know how many people will be in the room and how long the meeting is expected to last.)
- Will the temperature remain comfortable?
- Will air change sufficiently with doors and windows closed?
- Have all heating, air conditioning and fan controls been tested?

Light Control
- Can the room be darkened sufficiently?
- Can room lights be dimmed or switched independently?
- Are all light switches located, checked and labeled?
- Are power outlets hot when lights are out?
- Is the room dark enough for projection?
- Are room light responsibilities assigned?

Power
- Will enough 120-volt AC be available to run all equipment?
- Are outlets conveniently located or will extension cords be needed?
- Are outlets switched and fused separately from room lights? Are spare fuses and standby circuit breakers ready?
- Are all extension cords tied or taped? Are enough adapters available?

Acoustics
- Will sound carry to all parts of the room without an annoying echo?
- Will there be interference from noisy mechanical equipment or sounds outside the room?

Other Facilities
- Are there fire extinguishers?
- Is there a telephone?
- Is manager's office phone number on hand?
- Is there a first-aid kit?

Lectern
- Is the height comfortable?
- Has the script light been tested?
- Has glare been eliminated from stage lights or spots?
- Is mike placement okay?
- Is a pointer handy?

Doors
- Plan for people to come and go during the presentation.
- Is light from doors prevented from hitting screen?

Projectors

- Are the needed types of projectors availble with proper lenses, stands, cables, and reels?
- Are lenses and gates clean?
- Are they running okay?
- Is the sound system okay?
- Are there enough reels, magazines and carriers? Are they the right sizes? Is the condition okay?
- Have remote control cords and switches been tested?
- Are lenses the right focal length to fill the screen?
- Are vital spares on hand: lamps, belts, fuses, and repair kit?
- Is stand-by equipment ready?
- Have you considered taping alignment bars on the overhead projectors?

Booth or Projection Station

Do you have to erect a stand or move a table? If so —

Is it high enough to clear heads and hats?

Is it wide enough for all equipment?

Is it the right distance from screen?

Is it rigid and level?

Projectionists

- Will experienced projectionists be provided?
- What facilities will be available for remote control of equipment and/or communicating with the projectionist?

- Will a PA or sound-reinforcement system be needed? If so, plug in everything, then test it.
- Is PA working?
- Is feedback at working level?
- Is electrical interference or hum a problem?
- Is speaker placement okay?
- Are there enough PA mikes?
- Are mike cords long enough?
- Are mike stand heights okay?
- Is the tape recorder working?
- Has the recording mike been tested? (Remember, there will be less echo when the room is filled with people but the sound level will probably have to be set somewhat louder.)
- Will an experienced audio technician or operator be on duty?

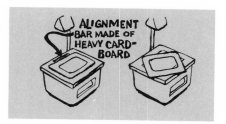

- Will you need a chalkboard, tackboard, display board or easel, extra tables for laying out presentation materials?
- What about supplies such as chalk, eraser, pointer, chart pad, markers and masking tape?
- Is everybody posted, checked out and cued?
  All equipment operators?
  Light-switch operators?
  Drape and curtain operators?
  Door guards?
- Are cued scripts for projectionist and audio man available?
- Are presenters checked out on mikes and controls?
- Is the schedule checked with the program chairman?
- Will you be providing a host for each meeting who will introduce the presenter?
- Have arrangements been made for signs to be made and placed to direct conferees to the meeting room?
- Do you need facilities and staff for simple production of last minute requests or advanced professional production for preconference preparation?

Mail presentation request forms to all participants a reasonable time in advance of the date of presentation (perhaps as early as six months in advance). Such forms should include all necessary information to expedite the provision of the facilities and services listed above. A suggested form is included in the Appendix.

Plan a time schedule which will give enough lead time for the best possible job of providing and coordinating these services. Also, anticipate last-minute crash requests.

In your schedule include regular dates for mailed reminders to insure that all requests come in early enough so that you will have adequate preparation time.

When requests are in and services have been assured, mail a final confirmation slip to the presenter at least two weeks before the presentation date. Follow this up with a carbon of the confirmation upon the presenter's arrival.

Arrange for a rehearsal with time and assistance to allow the presenter an opportunity to try his presentation in the space and with the equipment he will be using.

Give whatever support is necessary to the presenter in his actual presentation, making sure that he knows you are there to help in any way possible.

You may want to follow up the presentation with an evaluation questionnaire to determine whether the presenter feels he received all necessary support, e.g., equipment arriving on time, set-up properly made and in good operating condition. You might also canvass your audience to see whether they were satisfied with the arrangements.

SUGGESTED BASIC PRESENTATION STANDARDS FOR A PROFESSIONAL MEETING

The following standards are suggested as a basic beginning in levying requirements for all persons planning to give presentations at a professional meeting, conference or convention in order to achieve more consistently professional and effective presentations. These standards permit a first step toward building additional requirements in the future, when the members become more accustomed to the idea of uniform standards. The standards suggested here assume an essentially verbal orientation for the visuals, as this is where many persons will tend to begin. Future developments will see the presenters becoming more oriented toward picture as well as verbal presentation materials.

1. All presentations will be accompanied by projected visuals of some kind for purposes of audience orientation and retention. If you feel that your presentation does not lend itself well to visualization, please consider projecting the key outline points.

2. All slides and transparencies will be prepared for projection in a horizontal format, as this is more easily seen by the audience when they are looking over the heads of persons in front of them.

3. All lettering, formulae and diagrams will be copied as negative slides or transparencies for projection (white letters on black or colored background) in order to eliminate the background glare, dust and scratches usually seen in positive visuals. Such disturbances are distracting from the message of the visual. Lettering is to be done with an electric typewriter using a carbon ribbon on good bond paper and should be contained within a $2\frac{3}{8}''$ x $3\frac{1}{4}''$ frame for each visual. (A 3" x $4\frac{1}{8}''$ frame size can be substituted here. This frame is also useful in terms of general acceptable readability. The larger size does allow for more typing.) Type only with capital letters and double space between lines of typing. Try to limit the amount of wording in a frame. Do not fill each frame with words. Remember, each visual should work with you, not compete against you.

4. All photographs, cartoons, etc., will be copied as positive visuals for projection, as these items read better in positive form.

Appendix

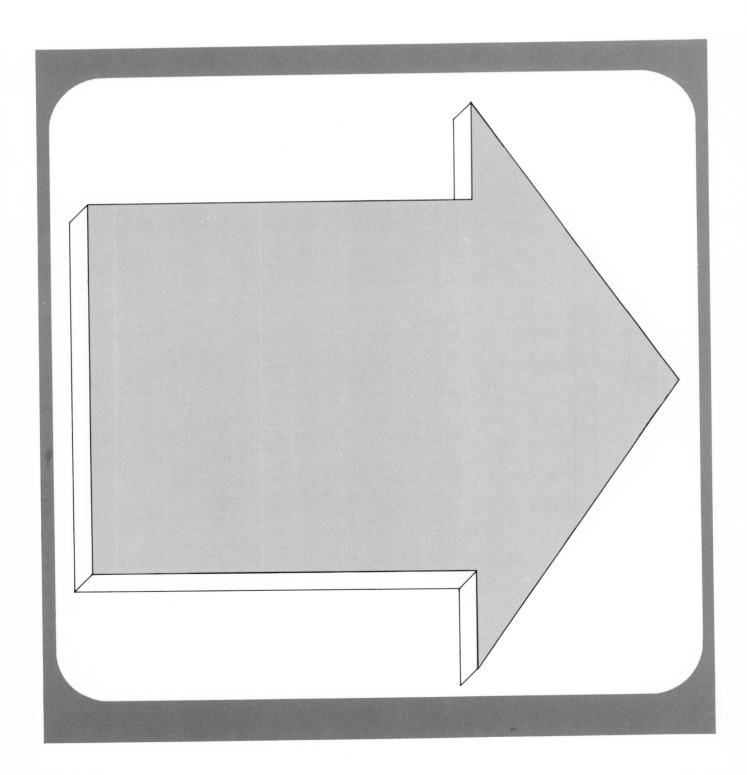

REQUEST FORM SAMPLE

Dear Program Participant:

Please fill out this form and return it within 10 days. Your needs for equipment to support your presentation at the Conference may be met more expeditiously if the information is available in advance to the Services Committee. Equipment will be properly selected and set up for your use in the normal operational mode if you will complete the following form and mail it to:

(Sponsor Representative Responsible for Service)
Address

Indicate the quantity of each type of equipment you require in the blanks below. A stamped addressed envelope is enclosed for your convenience.

_____ Overhead Projector, 10x10	_____ Filmstrip/Slide Projector
_____ Acetate Roll Attachment	_____ Opaque Projector
_____ 2x2 Slide Projector specify brand _____	_____ Record Player Audiotape Recorder/Playback
_____ 16mm Sound Projector	_____ Stereo
_____ 16mm Sound (Magnetic) Projector	_____ Monaural
_____ Sound Filmstrip System	_____ Magnetic Board type and size _____
_____ 8mm Projector type needed _____	_____ Flannelboard type and size _____
_____ 3¼x4 Slide Projector	_____ Television Equipment—attach sheet indicating brand, model and quantity of equipment desired

NOTE: A screen & projection stand will be provided with projection equipment.

Other equipment needed (easels, chalkboard, tables, other—specify size, if appropriate). _____

_____

_____

I will ( ) will not ( ) need the services of an operator.

Name:_____

Address:_____

Street Number   City   State   Zip

Telephones — Business:_____ Home:_____

— —

FOR SPONSOR USE: Session: _____ Time:_____

Date of Meeting:_____ Room/Bldg.:_____

ART PREPARATION AND
COPY TABLE

This table can be used in a variety of ways to produce visual materials which are transparent and projectable. Two production examples will demonstrate the use of the table. As you read the examples, refer to the table.

Example 1: You have a black and white print which must be made projectable for a fairly large group. A 2x2 slide is selected as the best conversion method for projection. A 35mm camera with color transparency film will be used to make color slides. (Lighting must be matched with the type of film used.) Even though your original photograph is black and white, color transparencies are more readily obtainable than are black and white with little significant difference in cost. Also, the color film gives black and white originals a slight color which is visually appealing.

Since slides are small, there is usually no practical means for adding information to them by hand after they have been made. (In the case of black and white line slides — negative or positive — color can be added by means of cellophane, plastic sheets or watercolor dyes.)

Example 2: A map line drawing (art) made with pen and ink (black) on bond paper can be converted to a transparency for an overhead projector by copying the drawing onto thermographic film. (No. 2 pencil could also have been used to make a copyable drawing.) Information can be added to the transparency with special fine-tip markers or color adhesive sheeting.

The transparency can also be made from the map drawing by shooting a high-contrast black and white negative. If the negative can be shot to the proper framing size for the overhead projector, it can be used directly for presentation. Otherwise, the negative must be enlarged to the appropriate size and printed on another sheet of high-contrast film. This second step results in a positive image. In both negative and positive image conditions, more information (coloring, words, lines) can be added as with the thermographic film visual discussed above. The high-contrast film will also accept watercolor dyes.

If your same map drawing is on a translucent-base material, such as tracing paper, the transparency can be made by copying on diazo film. The drawing can also be copied on color key film. Both films require ultraviolet light for printing. Diazo film gives a positive image and color key film gives a negative image. Both have a variety of colors available. (Color key has a double black film which gives a negative image very much like high-contrast film.)

SOME SUGGESTED ART PREPARATION AND COPYING METHODS FOR MAKING VISUALS

Original Picture (art or master)	Base Material on which original picture is made[1]	Means for Drawing, Lettering, Shading and Coloring the original picture	Copy Method for converting original picture into a visual	Size Change Flexibility Yes	Size Change Flexibility No	Visual[5]	Means of adding information to the visual
Continuous Tone (painting, illustration, photographic print)	Opaque (bond paper, cardboard, canvas, photo paper)	Any art medium	35mm photography: color	X		Slide	
			35mm photography: black & white (B&W)	X		Slide	Colored cellophane or plastic, water color dyes
Line (diagram, map, outline drawing, type or lettering)	Opaque (bond paper, cardboard)	Pen/black ink, No. 2 pencil Wrico, Leroy, speedball, special typewriter, special pasteup lettering and shading sheets.[2]	Thermographic		X	Transparency	As above. Add transparent color adhesive sheeting[3], pen/ink, fine-tip markers. Delete watercolor dyes.
			Electrostatic		X	Transparency	
			High-contrast photography (B&W)	X		Slide or transparency	As above. Add watercolor dyes.
			35mm photography (color or B&W)	X		Slide	See Slide (top)
	Translucent (tracing paper, frosted acetate)	As above. Add adhesive sheeting for coloring and shading, rub-down lettering.	As above. Add Diazo.[4] Add Color Key.		X	Transparency	See Transparency above
	Transparent (clear acetate)	As above. Add fine-tip markers; special marking pencils.[3]	None necessary, use directly as a transparency		X	Transparency	
Combination (base picture with one or more overlays)	Opaque, Translucent, Transparent	As above	35mm photography (color or B&W)	X		Slide	See Slide (top)

[1] Art requirements are approximately the same for motion picture, closed-circuit TV and lantern slides.

[2] If the thermographic copy method is used, the lettering and shading sheets must have a heat-resistant adhesive.

[3] Adhesive backing for transparent color and shading sheets must also be transparent in order to project satisfactorily.

[4] Add white opaque paper behind a translucent master for better printing contrast when copying by any other method than diazo.

[5] A slide is used in 2x2 or 35mm projector. A transparency is used on an overhead projector.

LETTERING AND LAYOUT GUIDE

This guide is provided as a useful method for making art to be copied for slide or overhead transparency visuals. Before you begin making the drawing, check to see whether the frame line matches the proportions of the actual projection frame opening of the slide (or transparency) into which you intend to mount your visuals. If you intend to copy the art on 35mm film for making slides, look at the guide through the frame opening of an empty slide or through the viewfinder of the camera to see to what extent the proportion needs to vary. Modify the guide proportions accordingly. Keep any information

inside a safety margin line ½" from your actual frame opening.

The guide can be taped to a larger piece of cardboard for a firm, ample working surface. Tracing paper can be positioned and taped over the grid. Drawing and lettering for copying purposes can be done on the tracing paper with a ruler and pen or marker. Preliminary layout lettering and sketching can be done with light blue pencil. None of the copy methods mentioned in the "Copying Methods" table will copy a blue line.

The guide lines (solid or broken) are spaced ¼" apart. Quarter-inch lettering is a safe, rule-of-thumb

height for this art size to insure that the projected image is readable by everyone in the room. Smaller sizes of lettering can be used depending on the importance of the information as well as the audience size and its distance from the screen.

An alphabet is given showing a hand lettering style recommended for uniformity and clarity. Hand lettering can be done with pen and ink, fine-tip markers or pencil. The height of the characters is two lines or ¼". Half-sized capitals can be used in some instances and still be readable.

ABCDEFGHIJKLMNOPQRSTUVWXYZ

1234567890.,-;'?&

abcdefghijklmnopqrstuvwxyz

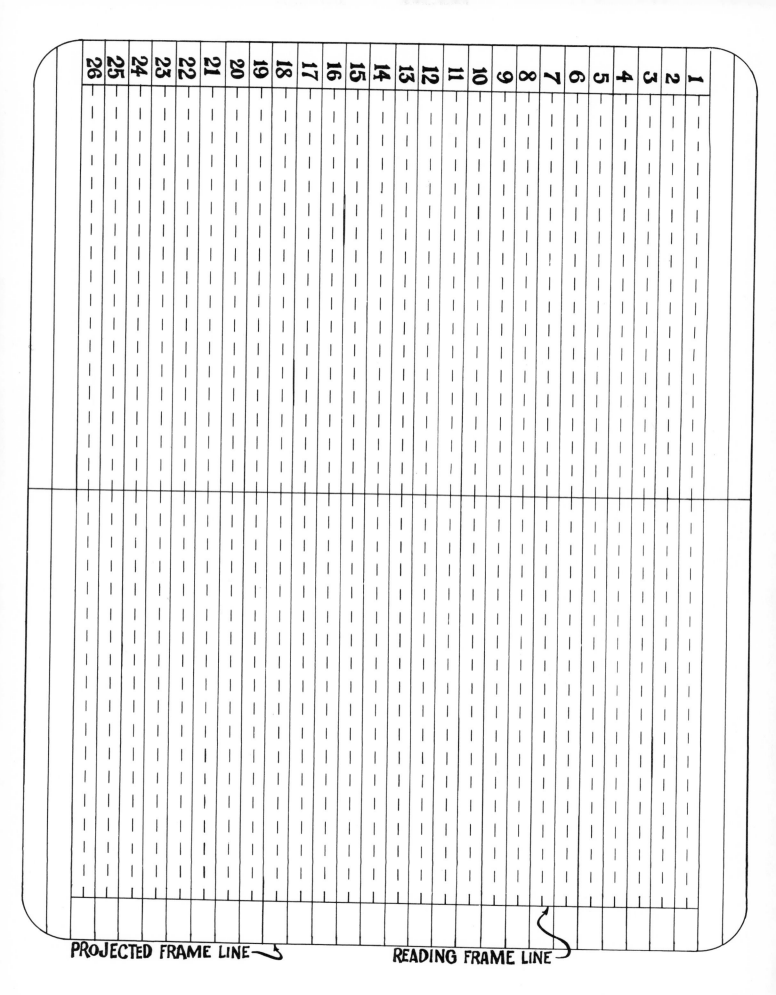

PROJECTED FRAME LINE ⤵

READING FRAME LINE ⤵

37

REPRODUCTION PROCESSES FOR PRINTING HANDOUTS

PROCESS	ART REQUIREMENTS	METHOD FOR MAKING TEXT	SUGGESTED NO. OF COPIES	COLORS	REMARKS
Thermographic	Draw directly on bond paper with black ink or No. 2 pencil	Type or letter on bond paper	1-10	Black only	Carbon-base black ink or pencil originals will print; colors will not
Electrostatic	"	"	1-100 depending on equipment	Black only	Colors, as well as black, will print
Spirit duplication	Draw directly on carbon master with ball point pen or stylus	Type directly on carbon master	Up to 150 depending on the master	Yes, up to five on the same master	Purple is the basic printing color. The black master tends to lose its clarity over 20 copies.
Mimeograph	Draw directly on stencil with stylus	Type directly on stencil	Up to 5,000 depending on the stencil	Yes, one color per stencil	Regular mimeograph (pictures are hand drawn on the stencil)
	Draw directly on bond paper with black ink	Type or letter on bond paper	same	Yes, one color per stencil	Electronic stencil mimeograph (pictures and typing can be pasted up together and cut into the stencil at the same time)
Offset	Paste drawings together with typed text	Type or letter on bond paper	unlimited	Yes, one per plate	Pictures and type can be pasted up together and shot on the same plate. Continuous tone pictures more easily and satisfactorily printed by this method. Size change is possible through photography.

SELECTED BIBLIOGRAPHY

Art-Work Size Standards for Projected Visuals, Kodak Pamphlet No. S-12. Motion Picture and Education Markets Division, Eastman Kodak Co., Rochester, N.Y. 14650. 8 pp. 1968. 15¢. It is both convenient and economical if artists producing originals from which projected visuals are made can adopt certain size standards. This pamphlet offers recommendations and provides a 3x4-inch template for photo prints or typewritten copy.

Audio-Visual Equipment Directory. National Audio-Visual Assoc., Inc., 3150 Spring St., Fairfax, Va. 22030. $8.50. Revised annually, this directory is a master reference to nearly all types and makes of AV equipment and accessories. The appendices include many useful charts, tables.

Audiovisual Literature Packet, Code No. U-915. Dept. 454, Eastman Kodak Co., Rochester, N.Y. 14650. $2.50. A convenient "instant library" containing about 30 Kodak publications — including several listed in this bibliography — on materials, equipment, techniques for filmstrip, slide, and motion picture planning, production and presentation.

Audiovisual Planning Equipment, Kodak Pamphlet No. S-11. Motion Picture and Education Markets Division, Eastman Kodak Co., Rochester, N.Y. 14650. 8 pp. 1969. 15¢. Gives specifications and suggested applications for three time-, money- and work-saving devices; a planning board, planning cards and a slide-sequence illuminator made from readily available, inexpensive materials.

Audiovisual Projection, Kodak Pamphlet No. S-3. Motion Picture and Education Markets Division, Eastman Kodak Co., Rochester, N.Y. 14650. 20 pp. 1969. 30¢. A compact reference for planning room facilities, seating plans, screen, speaker, and projector location, picture size, projector lamp and lens requirements, and other technical details which must be considered in putting on excellent audiovisual presentations.

Audio-Visual Trade Directory. National Audio-Visual Assoc., Inc., 3150 Spring St., Fairfax, Va. 22030. Single copy free. Listing dealers and manufacturers in the U.S. and Canada who are members of NAVA, this booklet indicates by a code the exact types of sales, service, film distribution, and equipment rental available from each dealer, together with complete addresses and telephone numbers for quick reference. Revised annually.

Better Communications Through Tape. Magnetic Products Division, 3M Co., St. Paul, Minn. 55101. 30 pp. plus tear-outs. 1968. Single copy free. A how-to-do-it guide book for more effective use of tape recorders. Includes detailed check-lists for recording meetings, conferences and special presentations.

DeJen, Gene. **Visual Presentation Handbook.** Oravisual Co., Inc., St. Petersburg, Fla.

Effective Lecture Slides, Kodak Pamphlet No. S-22. Motion Picture and Education Markets Division, Eastman Kodak Co., Rochester, N.Y. 14650. 8 pp. 1969. 15¢. Compares examples of slides which are good in design and legibility with those which are visually poor because of overcrowded content, lettering too small, or because the producer wrongly assumed that legibility on a printed page assures legibility on the screen.

Index to Kodak Technical Information, Kodak Pamphlet No. L-5. Professional, Commercial, and Industrial Markets Division, Eastman Kodak Co., Rochester, N.Y. 14650. 25¢. Lists alphabetically by both subject and by code number hundreds of currently available Kodak publications relating to photography and graphic presentation. Revised annually.

Kemp, Jerrold E. **Planning and Producing Audiovisual Materials,** second edition. Chandler Publishing Co., 124 Spear St., San Francisco, Calif. 94105. 252 pp. 1968. $8.50. A comprehensive basic reference to techniques for preparing picture series, slide sets, filmstrips, transparencies, graphics, sound recordings, motion pictures, and television materials. Glossary, bibliography and source lists for equipment, supplies and services.

Kodak Art Work Template, Kodak Pamphlet No. S-25. Motion Picture and Education Markets Division, Eastman Kodak Co., Rochester, N.Y. 14650. 8 pp. plus 2 templates. 1966. $1.00. Templates based upon an approximately 6x9-inch picture area show projected areas for single-frame filmstrips, 16mm motion pictures and 35mm slides and give recommended letter heights and line widths for various viewing distances.

Kodak Projection Calculator & Seating Guide, Kodak Publication No. S-16. Motion Picture and Education Markets Division, Eastman Kodak Co., Rochester, N.Y. 14650. 6 pp. 1969. $2.00. Consists of a table of seating capacities for rooms of various shapes and sizes and a three-part dial calculator interrelating the four key factors of image/screen size, frame size of transparency mask or projector gate, projector distance and lens focal length.

Minor, Edward and Harvey R. Frye. **Techniques for Producing Visual Instructional Media.** McGraw-Hill Book Co., 330 West 42nd St., New York, N.Y. 10036. 305 pp. 1970. $8.50. A comprehensive guide for producers of all types of visual media. Describes and illustrates familiar and practical graphic processes and newer, more complex production techniques. Extensive annotated bibliography and listing of sources for materials and equipment.

Morrisey, George I. **Effective Business and Technical Presentations.** Addison-Wesley Publishing Co., Reading, Mass. 01867. 143 pp. 1968. $4.95. Offers a systematic approach to the preparation and delivery of oral presentations and briefings. Includes suggestions for the use of different types of charts and other audiovisual materials.

Movies with a Purpose. Motion Picture and Education Markets Division, Eastman Kodak Co., Rochester, N.Y. 14650. 28 pp. 1968. 20¢. A clear and simple introduction to the planning, shooting and editing of short instructional or informational motion pictures. Emphasizes the importance of logical sequence of action, visual interest and continuity in films produced on a low budget.

Murgio, Matthew P. **Communications Graphics.** Van Nostrand Reinhold Co., 450 West 33rd St., New York, N.Y. 10001. 240 pp. 1969. $25.00. Explains the whys and hows of presenting data in understandable form. Covers charting techniques in great detail, keeping in mind the requirements of audience, presenter and facilities.

Nelms, Henning. **Thinking With a Pencil.** Barnes and Noble, Inc., New York, N.Y., 1964. $2.25. A book dealing with fundamentals of drawing with a pencil. The book was designed for (1) those who wish to use drawing as a tool for thought and communications but lack knowledge of how to make drawings and (2) those who are accustomed to drawing but want to enlarge their graphic vocabularies.

Planning and Producing Visual Aids, Kodak Pamphlet No. S-13. Motion Picture and Education Markets Division, Eastman Kodak Co., Rochester, N.Y. 14650. 16 pp. 1969. 25¢. Describes a "team approach" to the planning and production of audiovisual materials. Offers suggestions on scripting and titling, and describes some simple, but effective photographic techniques used by Kodak's Audiovisual Service.

Producers Manual. Magnetic Products Division, 3M Co., St. Paul, Minn. 55101. 43 pp. 1968. Single copy free. A concise, illustrated short-course in television production intended primarily for users of video-tape recording equipment. Glossary and bibliography.

Producing Slides and Filmstrips, Kodak Publication No. S-8. Motion Picture and Education Markets Division, Eastman Kodak Co., Rochester, N.Y. 14650. 56 pp. 1969. $1.25. Intended to help the small-scale producer of audiovisual presentations prepare professional quality slide sets and filmstrips with ordinary equipment. Emphasizes the use of the planning board and basic photographic and titling techniques.

Spear, James. **Creating Visuals for TV,** Publication No. 071-02630. National Education Assoc., 1201 Sixteenth St. NW, Washington, D.C. 20036. 48 pp. 1962. $1.25. Practical suggestions for improving TV programs through the more effective use of visual materials. Includes many ideas for projected and nonprojected resources and props and describes how to create special effects.

Wide-Screen/Multiple-Screen Presentations, Kodak Pamphlet No. S-28. Motion Picture and Education Markets Division, Eastman Kodak Co., Rochester, N.Y. 14650. 16 pp. 1969. 25¢. Discusses applications and various formats for wide-screen and multiple-screen presentations and shows how to produce visuals and employ one or more slide projectors to achieve dramatic special effects.

Professional Handbooks. Instructional Media Center, The University of Texas at Austin, Drawer W, University Station, Austin, Texas 78712.